# ME AND MY PLACE IN SPACE

by Joan Sweeney   illustrated by Annette Cable

Crown Publishers, Inc. ♛ New York

Also by Joan Sweeney and Annette Cable
*Me on the Map*

For the newest star in my universe, Keenan—J. S.

For Claire, Dena, Emily, and Isabelle, exploring these worlds together—A. C.

Published by Crown Publishers, Inc., a Random House company,
201 East 50th Street, New York, NY 10022

CROWN is a trademark of Crown Publishers, Inc.

http://www.randomhouse.com/
Printed in Singapore

*Library of Congress Cataloging-in-Publication Data*
Sweeney, Joan, 1930–
Me and my place in space / by Joan Sweeney ; illustrated by Annette Cable.
p.   cm.
Summary: A child describes how the earth, sun, and planets are part of our solar system,
which is just one small part of the universe.
1. Solar system—Juvenile literature.  2. Astronomy—Juvenile literature.  [1. Solar system.  2. Universe.]
I. Cable, Annette, ill.  II. Title.
QB501.3.S94                           1998
520—dc21                          97-16169
ISBN 0-517-70968-6 (trade)
0-517-70969-4 (lib. bdg.)
10 9 8 7 6 5 4 3 2

This is me on my place in space—the planet Earth.

Tonight, I can see the Moon from my place in space.

The Moon is a ball of rock that travels in a path around the Earth. Just like the Earth travels in a path around the Sun.

The Sun is really a fiery star,
as big as a million Earths.

So bright and hot,
it lights and heats . . .

. . . our whole solar system—nine different planets, including Earth, that travel around and around the Sun.

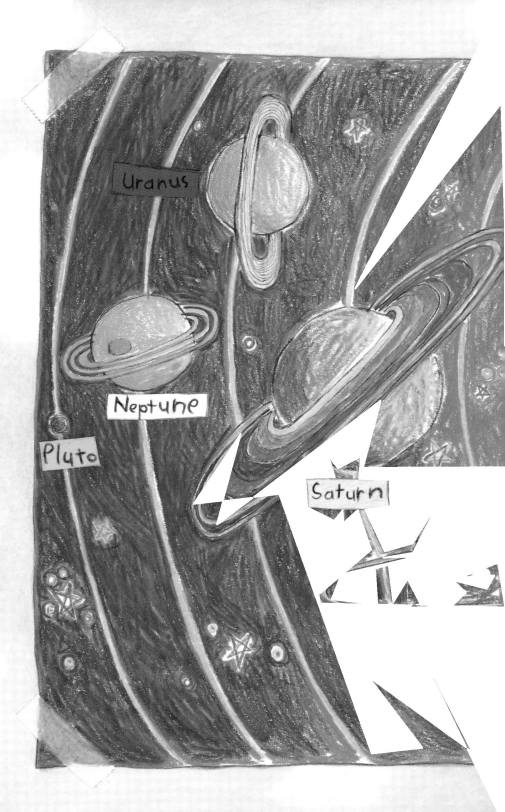

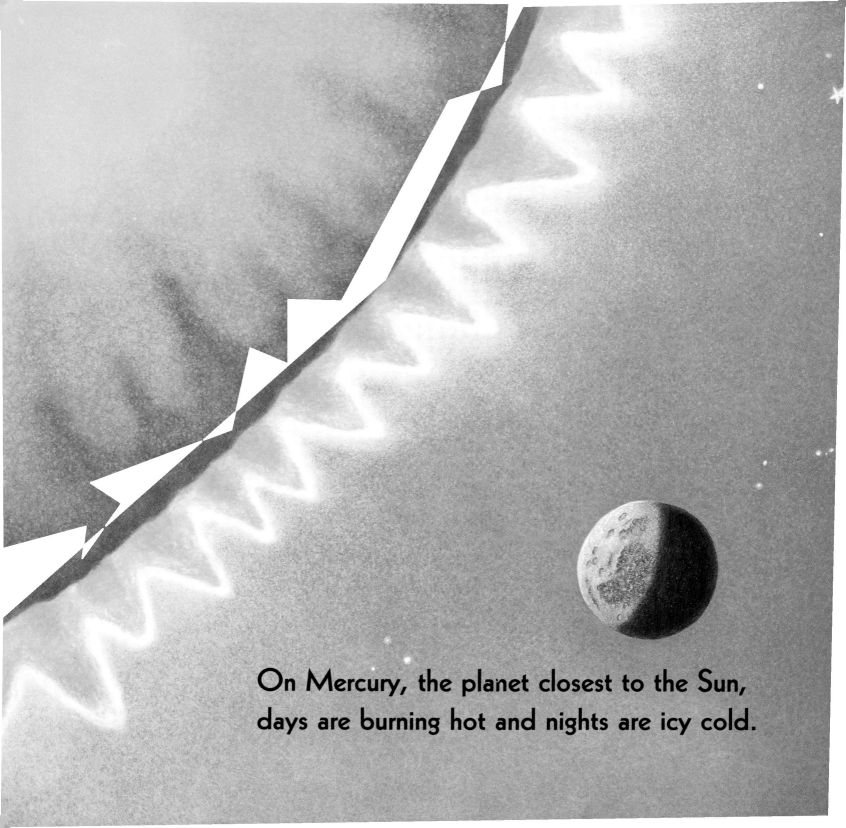

On Mercury, the planet closest to the Sun, days are burning hot and nights are icy cold.

The Sun comes up in the west on Venus.
Its gleaming cloud cover makes it the
brightest planet of them all.

My place in space—beautiful Earth—is the third planet
closest to the Sun. And the only one
in our solar system where
living things grow.

Long ago, there may have
been life on Mars. But now
Mars is rusty, dusty, and cold.

Jupiter is a massive ball of gas, bigger than all the other planets *combined*.

NEPTUNE
96,639

URANUS
99,742

SATURN
235,189

JUPITER
278,989

Saturn's wide rings are made of
ice particles, some big as houses!

On Uranus, it never gets warm, even though the Sun shines 42 years in a row!

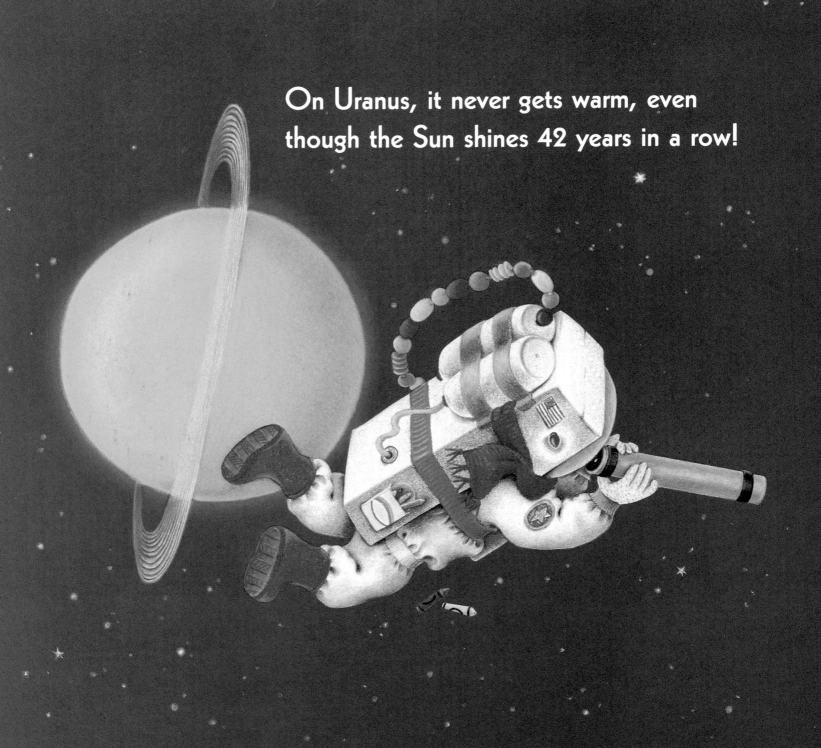

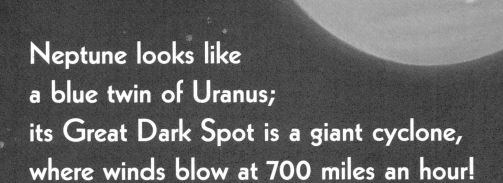

Neptune looks like
a blue twin of Uranus;
its Great Dark Spot is a giant cyclone,
where winds blow at 700 miles an hour!

And Pluto is an iceball so far away, the
Sun is like a dot in the distance.

But as big as our solar system is, it is only one tiny part of the Milky Way—an immense galaxy made up of hundreds of billions of stars, some with solar systems of their own.

And the Milky Way is only one of the many, many galaxies in the universe. So many, you might run out of numbers to count them!

And the universe is *sooooo* gigantic,
you could travel for trillions of years
and never get to the other side.

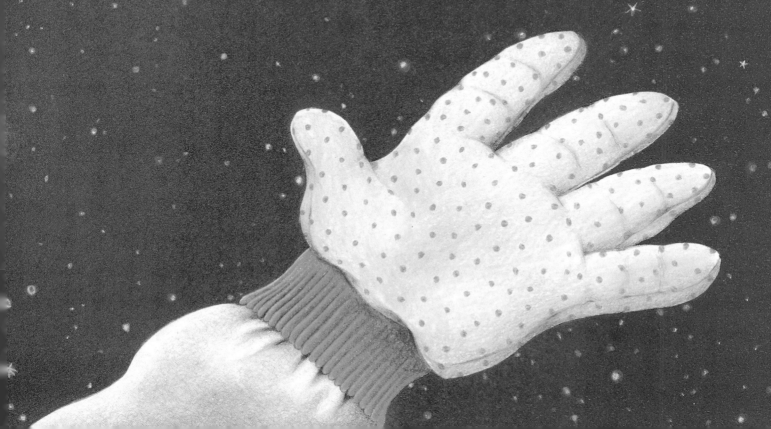

Sometimes I wonder.
Way out in space, is there
another galaxy like mine?

Another solar system like mine?

Another Sun like mine?

Another planet like Earth?

With another someone like me?

Could be.

# Words to Learn About Space

Galaxy: a group of many stars

Milky Way: the galaxy of which our solar system is a part

Moon: a ball of rock that moves around a planet

Planet: a ball of rock or gas that moves around a star

Solar System: a sun plus the planets that move around it

Star: an enormous ball of burning gas

Sun: a star that is at the center of a solar system

Universe: everything that exists in space